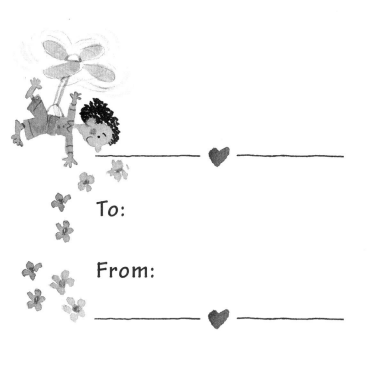

_____ ♥ _____

To:

From:

_____ ♥ _____

My mom's the best MOM

Compiled and Illustrated by Stuart Hample

WORKMAN PUBLISHING, NEW YORK

Library of Congress Cataloging-in-Publication Data
Hample, Stuart E.
My mom's the best mom / compiled & illustrated by Stuart Hample.
p. cm.
ISBN 0-7611-1968-X
1. Mothers—Miscellanea. 2. Mother and child—Miscellanea. 3. Children—Quotations.
I.Title
HQ759 .H228 2000
306.874'3—dc21   00-020555

Cover and interior design by Lisa Hollander with Jeanne Hogle

Workman books are available at special discounts when purchased in bulk
for premiums and sales promotions as well as for fund-raising or educational use.
Special editions or book excerpts can also be created to specification.
For details, contact the Special Sales Director at the address below.

Workman Publishing Company, Inc.
708 Broadway
New York, NY 10003-9555

Printed in Mexico

First printing February 2000
10 9 8 7 6 5

For my extraordinary mother, Helen Hample, 103 years young, born May 27, 1897, who has now lived in three centuries—the 19th, the 20th and—incredibly—the 21st!

Thanks to Janet Harris, mother of this book in many, many ways; to midwife Lisa Hollander; to Sally Kovalchick and Peter Workman, who lent serenity during birth. Thanks also to principals, teachers, parents and students at Beulah School, Columbia Grammar, Edgemont School, Manhattan Day School, P.S. 87, and Riverside School, and also to the kids we rounded up outside of classrooms.

CONTENTS

Introduction

INTRODUCTION

❤

In the beginning is Mom.

Mom nurtures her children in her womb, then provides culinary, domestic, and medical services, gives guidance, sympathy, understanding, and infinite love—without cease or conditions.

How these miraculous beings accomplish such prodigious feats, often while juggling a career outside the home, is known only to God. And to their children, whose thoughts, observations, and feelings about their mothers make up this book.

The respondents range in age from 8 to 13. No surprise, the main themes of their reflections are gratitude and love. But as might be expected, an obbligato bearing just a whiff of dissatisfaction may also be heard, because who else on the premises scrutinizes their every move?

The mix presents a portrait of Mom in many colors—droll, engaging, keen, honest, frazzled, and, of course, tender. It's a portrait that confirms what we have known since the beginning of time— mothers and children share a bond that is like no other.

—Stuart Hample

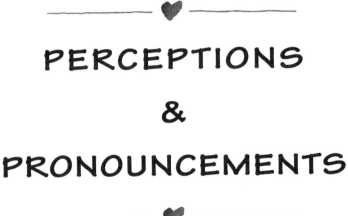

PERCEPTIONS

&

PRONOUNCEMENTS

Sometimes me and mom each read a book in the same room and we don't even talk.

It's one of the best times.

Justine, 12

My mom is teaching me to roller blade. It takes a lot of practis. But then she puts band aids on it.

Will - 9 yrs old

Before I go out I always ask her how do I look + she gives me her honest opinion. As opposed to my dad who always says you look gorgeous even if I look disgusting

Jackie, 13

My mom's hair is really brown, but she paints it blond.

Daniella, age 8

She comes to all of my basketball games. But she doesn't yell, she just smiles from her seat. And if I played rotten, she makes a joke or something after so I won't feel bad.

Steve, 10

My mom's the best
mom because she always
eats all the mushy bananas
so we get to have the new ones.

Gerald 9 3/4

My mom's French.
When something messes
up, she says merde.
But I know what she
means.

Claudine 10½

She says she drives extra careful when me and my brother are in the car because we are precious cargo.

Louis-9

When my mom gives me a sandwich she always makes the peanut butter go right to the edge with no bread showing because she knows that's the way I love it the most.

Alexis, $8\frac{3}{4}$

When I wanted a
sister she took that
into consideration.
So now I have one.

Flora, 10

I got adopted. But that's O.K. becuase my mom said they chose me over every other baby in the world

Douglas, 10

No mater how busy my mom is when she is cooking or at her desk, she always has time to talk to me or give me a hug.

Hallie, 6th grade

I like to look at pictures of her when she was my age and make believe we're best friends and know secret stuff we won't tell anybody else.

Cynthia (Cindi) going into 5th

When my mom goes away on a trip for her job, I get scared that she will forget me when she comes home. But she never did yet.

Stacey, 8

My mom says whoever took out the garbage without being asked I am very proud of you.

Andy, 9

She talks to our dog like he's a person. "Don't you DARE talk back to me." It's hilarious!

From, Dana, 12

When my mom cracked her favrite plate she cried. That made me cry. Then she started to laugh. Then I laughed too. Then she put the pieces in the garbage and said, "Oh well it isn't the end of the world."

Angelina
Age, 10

My mom loves me
as much as my dad
does. But not so
rough.

Timothy - 8 years
old

She is very nice to my dolls and stuffed animals. They love her almost as much as They love me.

Claudia, 8

I hope my mom could get her wish to be on Oprah, because she said she needs to express her feelings more. Maybe she could tell why she hates to cook.

Lindsay, 12

I go in our attic and put on her wedding dress and pretend I'm her when she married my dad. But if I was really her, I'd make him stop smokeing.

Anna, 11

Me and my mom played in the camp parents and kids game. The first time she got up the dads in the outfild moved in because they thought she can't hit. Then she belted one over there heads and were they suprised!

Denny, 9

CONCERNS, MISGIVINGS

&

CAVILS

If I'm out with friends I
have to call her at every stop.
Mom I'm okay. Are you having
a good time? Where are you?
Whos with you? She's like a detective.

Lukas, 13

My mom is also my piano teacher. she's a very good teacher but it's not fair because she lives there so she knows if I wouldn't practice.

Brenda, 9

She says she doesn't get angry. Ha!!!!!

Molly - 9

When I'm on the computer
and she wants to use it
She says she'll only be a
couple of minutes. But
it's always more like about
3 hours.

Candy 9 ½

My mom hates when I leave my clothes around. She says, "I'm not happy, Hannah!" So I pick them up because it's better for me when she's happy.

Hannah- age 11

I don't like it when Mom says I'm her "Favorite girl." I'm her only girl. But I love it when she says that I'm too tired to finish my homework.

Alexa

age 10

When my little brother bothers me, My Mother Just says you're the mature one, handle it how I'd handle it is i'd Mail him to Australia.

Rachel, 10

She made soup with about 2 million vegetables floating in it.

I said I hate it. She goes How do you know unless you try it?

I go I dont have to try something to know it's yucky.

Jonathan, 10

She's never accepted my opinion in 9 years.

Erica, age 9

When I'm a mother I won't sing along to songs on my daughters radio when I don't know the right words in front of all her friends.

Maren, 12

She reads the labels on _everything._
If it has chemical stuff with long names
she says it's poison. And she won't buy it,
no matter how much you beg.

Dianne, 9

She says yes when she needs to say yes, and no when she needs to say no. But I don't like to get kissed first thing in the morning.

Venessa 8¾

CERTAINTIES, APPRECIATIONS & ACCOLADES

She may not be perfect but I think she's as close to it as a mom can get.

Lola,
age 12

My mom works in the phone company and she took me two times for take your daughter to work. It was neat to sit on her desk and pretend I'm her boss (which she really is of me.)

Whitney, 9

When I'm upset my mother
Listens to me and comforts me
and says it's ok. Then it
always is

Vondelia, age 8 years

Its cool when she surprises me. Like she says she has a meeting then shows up at my soccer game. Its like getting a present when I didnt expect one.

Dylan, 10

I love it when my mom rents a movie if my dad has to work late. We cuddle up on her bed and eat a big bowl of popcorn. And if I fall asleep before it's over, she tells me how it turns out in the morning.

Emma, age 10

When we go out to eat
if I don't like what I
ordered she trades food
with me. It's lucky she's
my mom or I'd starve every
time.

Nick, 9 1/2

The top thing my mom does is when I have friends over keep my little sister out of my room. Definitely when I'm a mother I'm going to have only one child.

Rosa—10

When I get sick and have fever, my mom washes my face with a cool cloth. And whenever I wake up, she's there.

Julian 8 1\2 years old

My mother always 's thinking "What's best for Johanna? What would Johanna like?" And the best thing is, most of the time she's right.

Johanna, age 9 $\frac{3}{4}$

My mom lets me have my
cat Oliver even though
she's not a cat person.
But she's kind to
him anyway because
she knows I couldn't
live with-out him.

Patrica, 9

She sings to me when I'm going to sleep the ones she used to sing when I was little. They make going to bed nice.

Roland-8

My mom never embarasses me.
Like if I make a mistake
she always whispers it so
nobody else knows. Or when
she calls me her special
name for me, it's never
in front of any body.

Trish, 10

When she gets dressed up
really nice to go out at
night her perfume smells
so good and she's so happy,
I wish I could go with
them.

Kenny 8 $\frac{3}{4}$

Once on my birthday she gave me this huge wrapped box. Inside there was another box. Then smaller and smaller, and the last one had a penny in it. Then she gave me a necklace. She's really fun to be the child of.

Judith –
10

Everyone says that
their mom is the best,
but mine has a coffee
mug to prove it.

Jesse, 12½

She's so fun. If we eat in the Chinese restrant she always makes up what the fortune cooky says. Like I'll be the first one or become on Mars- a famous Opera singer.

Susannah, 9

My mom's beautiful as an emrald
and she's gentle as a dove. She's
nicer than anyone I know.
Without her nothing culd be worse.

Michael, 9

If I get a bad grade
she doesn't make a big deal.
She teaches me never to give up.
She went on the rollercoaster
with me when no one else would.
these are some of the
reasons I'm glad she had me
instead of somebody else.

Donald, 10½

I like when my mom thinks I'm asleep and she gives me a little kiss on my forehead and calls me her angelita pequeña.

Elena 9 1/2

I used to think she didn't pay attention to me, so she made a day just for me and her. We still do it and its so fun. But I love her everyday!

Neil, 13

She does good jokes.
Like on your half-birthday
she bakes a half of a
Cake and stuff like that.

Nicole, 9

My mom is the best
because she would
give me her gloves if
we were stranded on
a coldest iceberg in
the world.

Greg, Grade 3,
age 8.

She taught me how to do the bottom part of O Susana on the piano and she plays the top part. We played it for Nana and papa. They said it's better than anything on TV.

Teddy, 8

I love when she shampoos my hair and puts her curlers in it. When she's done she always says I could be a movie star.

Marcia, 9

Just being around her is Nice.

Josh, 8